INCREASING YOUR TWEETS, LIKES, AND RATINGS

MARKETING YOUR DIGITAL BUSINESS

SUZANNE WEINICK

ROSEN
PUBLISHING

New York

Published in 2013 by The Rosen Publishing Group, Inc.
29 East 21st Street, New York, NY 10010

Library of Congress Cataloging-in-Publication Data

Weinick, Suzanne.
Increasing your tweets, likes, and ratings: marketing your digital business/Suzanne Weinick.—1st ed.
     p. cm.—(Digital entrepreneurship in the age of apps, the web, and mobile devices)
Includes bibliographical references and index.
ISBN 978-1-4488-6928-2 (library binding)—
ISBN 978-1-4488-6976-3 (pbk.)—
ISBN 978-1-4488-6977-0 (6-pack)
1. Internet marketing. 2. Electronic commerce—Marketing.
3. Social media. I. Title.
HF5415.1265.W453 2013
658.8'72—dc23

                                                    2012006836

Manufactured in the United States of America

CPSIA Compliance Information: Batch #S12YA: For further information, contact Rosen Publishing, New York, New York, at 1-800-237-9932.

CONTENTS

INTROD

You are part of the generation that has learned to use Facebook, smartphones, Twitter, chat rooms, and blogs for multiple purposes in your everyday life. You probably don't remember life without contacting your friends online and surfing the Web. The world has changed in the way we communicate with each other and how we get information. According to the Pew Research Center, text messages and Twitter posts are the second most common methods of distributing news. Millions of people online debate the value of products and write reviews on everything from hotels and movies to computer games and mobile apps. Digital entrepreneurs need to learn to create a message about their products, spread the word, and field questions and comments about their creations.

UCTION

A digital entrepreneur is anyone who uses the Internet and mobile technology to create business opportunities. Many successful companies have been launched as Web-based businesses, and numerous products have been sold by Internet-only sales, marketing, and distribution. This means that you, too, can become a digital entrepreneur if you create something of value to the world and learn how to promote, sell,

Digital entrepreneurs are using mobile marketing to reach potential and existing customers. Marketing through e-mail, Web sites, blogs, and social media is the new way to get your message to the masses.

Smartphones, which put the Web and social media at people's fingertips at all times, are giving business owners new ways to connect and communicate with customers.

and stand behind it. Innovation and creativity are critical elements in marketing your digital business.

If you want to succeed as a digital entrepreneur, you need to create a strategy to use the tools available to you on the Web to sell your product to the world. Digital marketing is the process of using Web-based search engines, social media, and mobile devices to get your business message to potential customers. Your goal is to use diverse methods to connect with customers. These could include:

- Tapping into social media, for example, creating a Facebook page to promote your product

- Using search engines like Google, Bing, and Yahoo! to target customers based on gender, age, online activities, and past purchases

- Microblogging on Twitter about your product and offering incentives for purchasers

- Preparing a mobile marketing plan delivered via mobile devices

- Finding potential customers on the Web and collaborating with other businesses in your category of interest

Whether you are selling a product or service, all of these techniques can be used to make a sale. Digital marketing enables you to target your message to potential customers inexpensively and effectively.

Specifically, this book will focus on strategies for marketing digital products such as software applications ("apps") for smartphones, mobile tablets, and other devices. If you are an independent software developer creating apps for mobile computer devices, the strategies provided will assist you in getting your app noticed in a competitive market. However, whether you are selling mobile apps and games or a more traditional product or service, the underlying goals of marketing apply: to get your product noticed by your target audience.

CHAPTER 1

DIGITAL MARKETING

So you have created your own digital app. Now what? There are hundreds of thousands of apps already available on Apple's App Store and the Android Market, and more are being developed every day. This means that consumers have a world of choices about what apps to download to their mobile devices. Every app developer wants to get their app to the top of the "Staff Favorites," "New and Noteworthy," or "What's Hot" lists on the App Store. However, this is not an easy task considering the number of choices in the marketplace. As with any sale, marketing is the key to success, and mobile marketing is the new way to get a product noticed.

MARKETING PLAN

The goal of every app developer is to have consistent sales and positive feedback from purchasers. There are numerous ways to convey the value of your app and promote the special qualities of your app to potential buyers. Marketing is the important process of building and publicizing your unique message. However you choose to market your

An Apple store displays the icons of some of the thousands of apps available for Apple products. To generate "buzz" for your app or product, you will need a strong marketing plan.

digital product is up to you, but you need to have an overall marketing plan to stay organized and maximize your success. Developing your marketing plan takes a bit of work, but it will be worthwhile when your sales reflect your effort.

In his book *iPhone & iPad Apps Marketing: Secrets to Selling Your iPhone and iPad Apps*, author and app developer Jeffrey Hughes sets forth the simple steps to marketing a digital app: (1) create a marketing

LEARN FROM OTHERS

The only way to stand out from your competitors is to do something different. Review other similar apps in your category to determine what makes your app better. By learning the strengths and weaknesses of other apps, you will learn what to do to improve upon what is already available. Look outside your industry to discover creative ways to perfect your marketing message and draw attention to your product. Watch the "top applications" lists to see what apps are getting positive reviews and are being downloaded the most in different categories. Check out the Web sites of the application development companies to see how they promote their new products.

plan, (2) deliver your marketing message, (3) convert your prospects to customers, and (4) reuse your marketing plan. Specifically, you must identify and define your app's unique value and purpose. Then, you need to convey that message to the appropriate audience at the right time using the technology of your potential buyers.

There are a number of considerations you need to make when developing your plan. What is in an app's name? Naming your app will create a unique identity for your product. This is one place where you do not want to be too abstract or creative. You want it to be clear what your app is all about. Do your research by checking for other apps in the same category to see what similar apps are named. Describe the specific functionality of your app; this is key to your marketing message. If you place a keyword like "game" in the

Market seasonal apps with timing in mind. The launch of a holiday-themed game, like Christmas with Weezer from Tapulous, should occur in time to maximize preholiday downloads.

name of your app, this will indicate to the search engine where your app should be located in its directory.

Timing the release of your marketing information to go along with the posting of your app for sale is critical. For example, if you have an app that is related to a holiday (for example, Christmas lights for a smartphone), then November is a perfect time to launch your marketing and have the app available for sale. Also be aware that people tend to buy more apps right after they get a new smartphone, purchase a mobile tablet, or get other new technology that can accommodate apps.

While developing your app, keep in mind the target audience that would most likely find your app useful or enjoyable. You can achieve recognition for your mobile app by contacting publications in your audience's areas of interest. More generally, a review from a tech magazine such as *MacWorld* or *Wired* will give you national and international exposure.

CONNECTING STRATEGY

It is in your best interest to participate in the digital conversation and get closer to your potential customers. Your online connection with customers will create a network of possibilities for your business.

In today's digital world, you need to have an online presence by becoming an active member of several online social media networking services. Facebook, Twitter, Myspace, LinkedIn, and others are the social media sites that will enable you to reach your target audience. These online services allow you to e-mail members directly, post information, and find others who share your interests. They are great ways to generate free publicity for your product.

Once you have a digital app on the market, either for free or for sale, you will need to monitor online

Ad Board

Create

Own the Streets

Click here to play Mobsters and grow from petty thief to Mafia Don. Run the street, build your mob, be the boss!

Manhattan's Daily Deal

We offer 1 ridiculously huge coupon each day. Restaurants, spas, tickets and more for 90% off. Come see today's monster deal!

Bloomberg employee?

NY Dental Spa offers Bloomberg employees with ppo dental ins. a whitening, cleaning, and exam for only $1.00 out of pocket! Click now!

News on Biz Journalism

Your daily resources for staying up to date on the world of business and economics journalism.

Let Rodney Rescue You

He's ready to take you to Ocean City, Maryland. Me him now at www.ococean.com.

US-ASEAN Creative Project

Accepting Early-bird submission for 2009 Short Films Competition! Win US$1,000.00

Everyone plays Mafia Wars

Play the game millions of people play each day with their friends. Do jobs, embezzle cash, fight your rivals. You are the

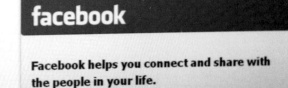

Welcome to Facebook! | Facebook - Mozilla Firefox

File Edit View History Bookmarks Tools Help

facebook

Facebook helps you connect and share with the people in your life.

Facebook is a good platform for both paid ads and word-of-mouth advertising. If people "like" your Facebook page or use your Facebook app, their friends will learn about your product.

conversation about your product. Hopefully, you will receive direct feedback from your customers on your Web site. You need to listen to what your customers say about how your product works, and you will have to respond to questions and concerns. If you foster a positive environment for interaction with your customers, you will create loyalty to you when your next app is available.

APP GONE VIRAL

Make sure to include a function within your app that gives users the opportunity to recommend your app to their friends. If your app is a game, include the ability to play with friends, usually called a multi-player function. You may even be able to integrate group interaction through Facebook, Twitter, and other social media sites. This will enhance the experience for the user of your app and also expose new customers to your product. Facebook Connect allows application developers to connect with Facebook through the app once it is downloaded. When someone gets a high score on a game that is linked with Facebook Connect, the information is sent to the user's Facebook page as a "News Feed" or "Status Update" post. This gives your app exposure on Facebook and encourages other people to play.

IT STARTS WITH YOUR WEB SITE

Digital businesses increasingly rely on Web-based marketing and communication to reach potential customers. It's a good idea to start a company Web site where you can showcase your app or other product. On your Web site, you can show your app in action through video and slideshow visuals. This will catch the attention of potential users and illustrate the value of your product. User testimonials are another great way to show that your app is a good product to own.

Most people search the Web for specific content, and they use a search engine, like Google, Yahoo!, or Bing, to find what they are looking for. Once people do a search and retrieve the results, they usually look at only the first page of listed sites and blogs. Therefore, if your Web site or blog is not listed on the first page of a search engine's results, people may never see your site listed. Therefore, you need to take steps to raise your ranking and increase your Web site or product's visibility in searches. This is known as search engine optimization (SEO). There are many tools on the Internet to assist you in SEO techniques, including choosing keywords that best describe your product, service, or the content of your blog or Web site. SEO strategies are often free to implement. However, it is often difficult to get your Web site, product, or blog noticed on popular search engines without paying your way to the top of the Internet search.

Paid search engine marketing (SEM) is advertising on a search engine, such as Google or Yahoo!. In paid SEM, the search engine's advertising service (such as Google AdWords or Yahoo! Advertising Solutions)

Your business's Web site is crucial for communicating the value of your product. Positive reviews and user testimonials can help reinforce your message and enhance your product's appeal.

places a well-targeted, short, text-based ad on the search engine site. The ad appears when a Web surfer enters a search phrase that matches a list of keywords related to the product. This type of online advertising is targeted and cost effective.

According to *Entrepreneur* magazine's book *Start Your Own Blogging Business*, the best thing about paid search advertising is that you pay only when someone clicks on your ad to reach your Web site, blog, or other online presence. Otherwise, if a surfer sees your ad but does not click on it, you don't pay for the search that showed your ad. This is known as pay-per-click (PPC). The exact cost to the advertiser is known as the per-click rate.

PRESS RELEASES

To draw more attention to your new product, you can create a press release to announce the availability of your app. A press release is a tool used to inform the media about developments in your company. You should send your press release to publications, bloggers, and Web sites that target your audience. Again, knowing your target audience is critical to getting your message to the right people who will be interested in your product.

It is essential that your press release is written carefully and that it provides all the necessary information. A well-drafted description of your app is critical in helping searchers find your app in the marketplace. It is wise to get help from friends, teachers, or writers to edit and review your press release before you send it out. Otherwise, there are online press release sites that will proofread and edit your press release for a fee.

Media outlets and bloggers use press releases to provide the background material they need to write their reviews of new apps or products. Therefore, your press release needs to include:

- A detailed description of the app/product and its unique features

- A brief history of your company and development of the app

- Links to your Web site, Facebook page, etc.

- Images or screen shots of your app

- Contact information: your e-mail address, phone number, and Web address

Once you have been given a release date for your app from the App Store or Android Market, you can send out your press release a few days or a week before.

CHAPTER 2

BLOGGING AND MICROBLOGGING

B logging is a means of posting content and communicating with others about it on the Internet. It allows anyone with an Internet connection the ability to share ideas, knowledge, and information immediately. Blogging has become so popular that there are even blogging directories, such as Technorati, that index blogs by category. Blogging can be a very cost-effective promotional tool to get your marketing message to the masses.

THE POWER OF BLOGS

From a business standpoint, there are two distinct ways to use blogs to promote and sell your product or service. One is to create your own blog to inform the public about your area of expertise. The second is to reach out to professional bloggers and have them review your product or app. In either case, blogs can be used to communicate your message online for free.

If you are an independent app developer, you should establish a relationship of trust with professional bloggers before reaching out to them to review your app. Show bloggers in your field of interest that you are a professional and that you have knowledge of the subject matter being discussed. There are many individuals who blog about mobile apps on a regular basis. You should follow their blogs so you will know in advance if they might be able to put out a good word about your app. Once you know bloggers that are likely to be receptive to your product, send them a "sneak preview" of your app before it is available online. This will be an incentive for them to check out your product and give you feedback.

You can also set up your own free blog to promote your apps. Your blog posts can be linked to your Facebook and Myspace profile pages. Videos and graphics can be posted to your blog to give potential customers a taste of what your app is all about. But note, having your own blog means that you will have to blog on a regular basis in order to keep followers engaged. Maintaining your own blog is a big time commitment. You need to constantly think of and create new content for your blog in order to generate traffic on your site. Successful blogs are those that are creative and understand what the target audience wants and needs from the specific site. You will need to be patient and persistent in amassing a group of dedicated followers and increasing your online traffic over time.

ENTERING THE TWITTERVERSE

Another popular place on the Web for a business to get noticed is Twitter, a popular microblogging service. On its Web site, Twitter defines itself as a "real-time information network." Small businesses are already

Blogs empower people to express their knowledge and opinions to others with similar interests. For this reason, bloggers can have a strong influence on your digital business's future.

realizing that 140-character "tweets" can have an impact on consumers.

Twitter offers an entrepreneur a creative way to establish an identity for an app or product. According to Dennis Prince, author of *Get Rich with Twitter*, tweeting gives you the opportunity to tell customers "what you offer, how you offer it, and how you listen to those who like or dislike it." The art of the tweet is that it delivers your message in a short burst of infor-mation. The goal is to provide a relevant message without losing your audience's attention.

Prince recommends creating your Twitter account thoughtfully, especially if you are entering the Twitterverse (the world of those using Twitter) with the goal of enhancing your business. When selecting your Twitter name, also referred to as a "handle," make sure it is simple and easy to remember. It is a good idea to choose a name that is similar to the Web site or business name that you have already established. Provide a profile photo or image when you set up your Twitter account. The image can be your logo or a picture that represents your business or app category. Everything that you put on Twitter is part of your business's public persona.

Your Twitter account can be linked to your mobile phone, giving you flexibility to send and receive tweets from anywhere. From the Twitter home page, you can manage your account and see how many followers you have. If you are going to use Twitter to promote your business, you need to tweet regularly— at least once a day is preferable. If you tweet too often, some followers will be turned off and "unfollow" you on Twitter. You want to allow time between your tweets to encourage responses from your followers.

It is important to tweet interesting information or to be humorous so that your followers stay engaged. Asking people to contribute feedback or helpful hints on using your app are great ways to increase your tweets from followers. You can also include links to your Web site and/or blog in your tweets. If your app or product receives a favorable review from a trade or

VIDEOS AND VLOGGERS

A great way to get your app or product noticed on the Web is to post a YouTube video. YouTube is free and relatively easy to use. Advertisers know that people would rather see what your app is really like than read something about it. YouTube videos should not exceed two minutes in length and should demonstrate the virtues of your app. Make sure that you tell consumers where to go to purchase or download the app.

Don't feel like you have the right stuff to make your own video? Try using a professional vlogger. Vloggers are people who post video regularly on the Web. If you check out YouTube and search a topic, chances are you will find popular vloggers with huge followings. Many vloggers are entertaining and informative on the topic they are vlogging (video blogging) about. Successful vloggers can make money from their posts by creating a unique YouTube channel and by becoming a YouTube partner.

online publication, you can link to it in a tweet to spread the good news to your followers.

Note that tweets can be posted to all of your followers, directed to a specific group of followers, or sent privately to one follower. If someone complains about your app, you may want to respond directly to him or her and then follow up with a general response to all of your followers once you have resolved the problem.

MANAGING YOUR TWEETS

It is not easy to manage all the social media sites when starting a new business. There are many tools popping up to help you monitor traffic on the Internet and assist you in keeping the information flowing. A very useful online service called SocialOomph (https://

Twitter is all about what is trending right now. Used effectively, Twitter can help create a following for your product and get people engaged with your company.

www.socialoomph.com) allows you to set up tweets in advance and schedule them to appear at a specified date and time. This service has free and paid options and is an easy way to stay organized and current with your tweets. SocialOomph also gives you the ability to automatically follow people who are following you.

There are Twitter tools that allow you to create a blog post from each of your tweets (for example, at the blogging Web site WordPress.com) and ones that translate your tweets into other languages. Kevin Rose, founder of Digg.com and a Twitter expert, suggests that you follow some top Twitter users to see what they tweet. You can learn from seeing how other entrepreneurs use Twitter to promote their businesses and products. For example, you can check out Kevin Rose on Twitter to see a well-organized bio and links to his business ventures.

Beware that some people will follow your Twitter stream with the motive of increasing their own Twitter follower count. If you realize that some of your followers are not truly interested in your content, you can block them from your tweets. As pointed out by Dennis Prince, while this is the reality of Twitter, your goal is to "develop a following that's truly suitable to your purpose." There should be a beneficial relationship between you and your followers.

CUSTOMER INTERACTION ON TWITTER

Jack Dorsey, one of the creators of Twitter, was motivated to create a Web-based immediate communication tool for the taxi industry. Now, businesses large and

FULL DISCLOSURE

The Federal Trade Commission (FTC) issued new guidelines that require that anyone blogging, tweeting, or otherwise publishing on the Internet about brands or products must disclose if they are being financially compensated in exchange for providing such information. Failure to do this fits the definition of deceptive advertising; failure to disclose is an omission that can mislead consumers and influence their decisions about a product or service. The FTC can issue a fine to any company that does not monitor and disclose that reviewers or bloggers are being paid to provide favorable information about a brand, product, or service. Advertisers must comply with the FTC rules as well.

small are using this microblogging site to interact with customers and provide them with useful information in a concise manner. If you create an update to your app, send a tweet to advise your customers where to download or purchase the update once it is available.

Twitter can be useful to generate awareness of your product or app. Keep the tweets professional and only provide personal information that is of interest to your target audience. Whatever you post, realize that everything you say will be a part of your public image for a long time. Remember, there are search engines for social media outlets that track all posts. Services

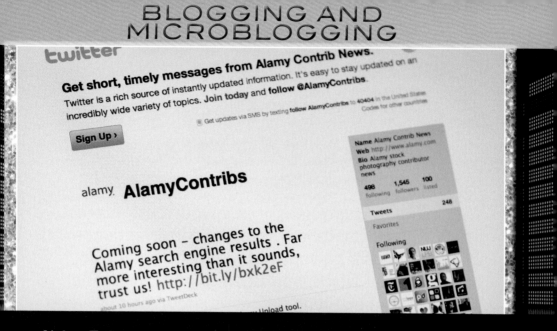

Using Twitter, you can let your customers know about your latest product enhancements and updates. Capture their interest with witty, informative blurbs of relevant information.

such as Tweet Scan (http://tweetscan.com) are a way to search the Twitterverse to see what is being said about your product. If you register with Tweet Scan, you will receive an e-mail notification every time your search term, brand, or product is mentioned on Twitter. Tweet Scan is a way to monitor complaints about your product or service and perform damage control.

The most important thing to remember about marketing your app or product on Twitter is to be creative. Think of a few catchphrases that describe how users will benefit from incorporating your app into their lives. A tagline that sums up your app's purpose in one line is the key to successful Twitter marketing. Digital marketing on Twitter is getting the buzz out on your app or product. It is inexpensive and can be fun.

CHAPTER 3

CONNECTING VIA SOCIAL MEDIA

As an entrepreneur, it is in your best interest to participate in the digital conversation and get closer to your potential customers. In today's digital world, you need to have an online presence by becoming an active member of several online social media networking services. Facebook, Twitter, Myspace, LinkedIn, and others are social media sites that will enable you to reach your target audience. These online services allow you to e-mail members directly, post information, and find others who share your interests. They are great ways to generate free publicity for your product. Facebook is the most popular of the social networks, but all of them give you access to large groups of people with specific interests.

Online social media, chat rooms, and blogs are forums for like-minded individuals to communicate and collaborate. People are going on the Internet to discuss their favorite music, share travel advice, and find the best places to eat Indian cuisine in Portland, Oregon. This means you can find people who are talking about whatever category your app or product fits into. Exchanging ideas, offering advice, and

Mark Zuckerberg's concept for Facebook was to connect friends through an online social network, but many companies are now using the site as a marketing tool.

participating in the conversation are great ways to establish a name for yourself as a respected app developer and as a mentor to others in your field of interest. Not only will you help your potential customers, but your online connections will also give you important information to achieve success.

FACEBOOK PAGE BASICS

Facebook is the most popular of the social networking sites, with more than eight hundred million users and counting. Facebook is based on the idea of sharing information by connecting with "friends" in an online community. It started out as a way for individuals to connect with each other, but it has evolved into a forum where businesses, organizations, places, brands, and products also gain access to the social network. This means that businesses can use the power of social media to create a business page, host an event, advertise a new product, and buy and sell merchandise.

A business profile on Facebook is called a "page." It contains basic company information, logos, products,

Companies like Coca-Cola are creating Facebook pages to market their products, and you can, too. Facebook even provides a template for small businesses to create a public page. Link the page to your business's Web site.

upcoming events, photos, and links to the company Web site. Unlike your personal Facebook profile, a Facebook page representing a company, brand, or organization can automatically accept "fan" requests and is not restricted to a limit of five thousand friends. Since marketing is all about finding potential customers, creating a personalized company page is a good idea for every business. The best part is that you can create a company page on Facebook for free.

As explained in *Facebook Marketing for Dummies* by Paul Dunay and Richard Krueger, the company page "allows a two-way conversation between a business and its customers." Facebook pages are publicly available, and therefore search engines, such as Google, can index them. This means they will show up on search results with your company's name or keywords. You can also use Facebook to send a message in the form of a "status update." These status updates will show up on your fans' "news feeds" and will give your company and product publicity.

One of the most important steps in creating your business page on Facebook is to select the proper category that best describes your company or product. Also note that once you create a name for your page and get more than twenty-five fans, you can claim a vanity URL on Facebook. Your company page can also be customized with Facebook applications. Once you have created a page for your company or product, you should post a message on your personal Facebook profile and invite your friends to become a fan of your business page. When members of Facebook discover your page, they can click "Become a Fan" to be added to your list of fans. The exciting part is that once people become fans, their friends see that they have become fans of your page on their news feeds. Starting this cycle can help generate interest in your page.

JOIN THE CONVERSATION

You probably already have your own Facebook personal profile. Just by connecting with your high school class-

Convert your existing customers into Facebook fans, and use the platform to target future customers. Add pictures and video of your products and share news about your business to engage people. Encourage people to join in the discussion.

mates and other family and friends, you have started a network of contacts. These people will be your initial support for any business venture that you launch. Do not be afraid to tap into these contacts and let them know about your new business project or product.

Your Facebook "wall" is where you can continuously update your information with posted messages, links to Web sites, photos, and video feeds. Posting on your wall is a great way to publish information about your product. You can use links to your Web site and any news coverage you receive by posting them on your wall. Your wall posts will also show up on your friends' news feeds. This will create instant publicity for what-ever product or service you are selling. Books such as *Facebook Marketing for Dummies* can walk you through the steps of creating a Facebook page and explain how to use Facebook to market your product or app.

Facebook "groups" are groups of people on Facebook who share an interest in a particular topic, hobby, or interest. If your mobile app has a target audience with one or more Facebook groups, it is a good idea to encourage them to review and comment on your product to spread the word. Remember, Facebook and all social networking sites are about making connections.

The downside to all this connecting is that you need to be honest and open when communicating with fans, cus-tomers, and critics. There are certain rules of etiquette that need to be followed when sharing information on

FACEBOOK MARKETING ETIQUETTE

Your wall on Facebook (or your business page on other social media sites) should be a place that reflects well on you and your business. Always keep your responses professional. Do not say anything online that could be considered inappropriate or rude. If you need to respond to a negative comment made about your business or product, do so politely and with facts. You do not have to respond to someone who is irate or disrespectful. Also, be conscious of the fact that Facebook is primarily a social networking site for personal communications. If you become too intrusive and bombard your target audience with marketing, your "friends" may tune out your message in the future.

social networks. For example, you should never be defensive or nasty when responding to customer criticism.

MONITOR THE FEEDBACK

Facebook, like all social networks, is a two-way medium. This means that you can start the conversation about the attributes of your product, but you will need to respond thoughtfully to positive and negative feedback.

It is important to turn customers into "fans" of your app or product. Disappointed critics will cause damage to your reputation if you do not react appropriately to their concerns.

Facebook has an internal instant-message feature and a message link. Use these to respond immediately to your customers. Your business page can be customized to attract new customers and offer promotions to those who become a "fan" of your page. Continuously update your Facebook page to attract more fans.

A survey on your Facebook page is an efficient way to collect information about your app or product. A survey is a method of gathering data from your target audience so you can improve your product. Marketers have been using surveys for years. With an online survey, you can engage your customers in evaluating your product and providing valuable information for future updates. Keep your questions short and simple. Do not give more than four choices per question. Be sure to thank those customers who complete the survey.

Your online connection with customers will create a network of possibilities for your business. Monitoring the user experience through social networking sites is a great way to see the impact of your app or product on your target audience.

FACEBOOK APPS

Facebook provides the tools for users to create their own apps using the Facebook platform. Any Facebook app can be integrated with your Facebook page. When someone uses a Facebook app, it generates a "story" that appears in the news feed of the person using the app. All the "friends" of that user see the story on their Facebook news feed.

Developing Facebook apps can be a business in itself, or it can help you increase sales for another type of business. For example, the restaurant chain Pizza Hut created a successful Facebook app that allows customers to order pizza while on their profile page.

MARKETING ON SOCIAL MEDIA SITES

All app developers want purchasers to be their "friend" on Facebook and to be "liked" by all customers. However, since social networking sites are constantly being bombarded with advertisements and national brand pitches, it can be difficult for independent app creators and small businesses to make their mark. In addition, with all of this digital marketing to Facebook users, it appears that most people on Facebook are not interested in interrupting their conversations with their real "friends" to make friends with a product or brand. In his book *The On-Demand Brand*, author Rick Mathieson notes, "Out of the over 600,000 branded pages that Facebook Page Tracker monitors, a mere 57,000 have more than 1,000 'fans.'" This leads to the conclusion that the big consumer brands are having a hard time entering into the Facebook conversation.

To promote its Facebook app, Kodak kept an actor and his photos inside a Plexiglas box until one million photos were "freed" from Facebook. Think outside of the box when promoting your product!

However, if you keep your promotion limited to your relevant customer base, you may find some genuine "friends" through social media.

If you want to create real interest in your app in an online community, you need to interact with your consumer base in a meaningful way. Mathieson says you need to spark the conversation by actively providing information related to your area of expertise. This will give you credibility with your prospective customers.

The goal is to spread your message while interacting with new "friends" and "fans."

Overall, social media is vital to any business because it is where your peers are hanging out to find out what to buy and where to get it. Facebook, Twitter, and LinkedIn are places on the Web where people can locate your company or product. Social media is a great way to share information with your target audience without the traditional costly forms of advertising and marketing.

CHAPTER 4

MOBILE MARKETING

Smartphones and tablets are mobile devices that can be used for many different purposes. In addition to making phone calls, communicating via video chat, and playing games, people use them to surf the Web, download and enjoy music and media, send e-mails and tweets, and connect to social media. Smartphones are preinstalled with operating systems that run the programs and applications.

According to Facebook.com, more than 425 million active Facebook users access the social networking site through their mobile devices. Many companies are creating advertising in the form of games and apps. Advertisers are discovering that reaching potential consumers through smartphones, called mobile marketing, is the new generation of advertising.

MOBILE SEARCH ENGINES

More and more people are using their mobile devices to search the Web. They want immediate information that is easy to read on these smaller screens. In order to increase your mobile Web traffic, you need to make sure that your mobile Web site is ranked well in mobile search engines. Mobile search engines

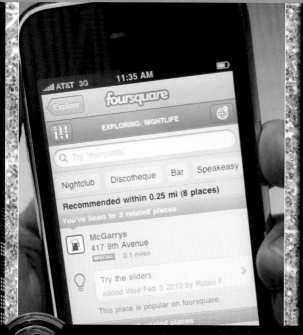

Increasing numbers of mobile users are surfing the Internet, checking Facebook, tweeting on Twitter, and searching Foursquare on their smartphones and tablets. Sales opportunities on the mobile Web are expected to keep growing.

evaluate your site based on how it displays on a mobile device and then rank those results. This affects your Web site rank when there is a search query that connects your mobile Web site with keywords in the search. Improving the quality of your users' experience and increasing your visibility in these searches is known as mobile search engine optimization (MSEO).

The art of mobile Web site development can be complicated, but there are resources available to help you make your mobile Web site user-friendly on mobile devices. Check with Google, Yahoo!, and Bing on MSN for information on properly formatting your mobile Web site to achieve optimum viewing.

MOBILE ADVERTISING

To take your marketing to the next level, get your business message out through banners displayed on mobile devices. When people surf the Web, engage in social networking, or play games using mobile applications on their smartphones or tablets, advertising banners appear. These advertisements give a brand or product exposure to new customers. The goal is to get your app or product noticed on the mobile devices that your potential customers are using.

There is a cost to this type of advertising. Businesses often pay on a pay-per-click (PPC) basis. They pay a certain rate for each time the advertisement is "clicked" and the user is sent to the company's Web page or to a downloaded advertisement. In another model of advertising, known as cost per mille (CPM), businesses pay a rate for a certain number of appearances of an ad, usually one thousand views. Users viewing the ad do not have to click or take other action.

When designing your mobile advertising, you should think of creative ways to get your product noticed. Take a look at what other companies are doing. When you search the Web from your smartphone, what ads draw your attention? It may be the graphics, text, or animation that gets you to read an ad or that makes you want to "click" to find out more about a product.

Cindy Krum, a mobile marketing consultant, believes that mobile marketing is uniquely personal. In her book *Mobile Marketing: Finding Your Customers No Matter Where They Are*, she says that the cell phone "is the most personal piece of technology that most of us will ever own." Unlike landline phones and

WI-FI IN THE AIR

According to the Web site ZDNet, in 2012 and beyond consumers will see big developments in in-flight Wi-Fi on major airlines. The airlines are installing satellite-based Wi-Fi systems on planes, and fliers will pay for the ability to stay connected in the skies. This means that you will soon be able to tweet, e-mail, surf the Web, and download the latest app while flying at 35,000 feet (10,668 meters). Jaunted.com reports that a company, Skycast Solutions, has developed a tray table laptop that will have a touch screen at every seat. This is an aviation breakthrough since most flyers are used to being instructed to turn off the Wi-Fi function of their electronic devices during flights. This new development means expanded opportunities for those marketing digital products.

desktop computers in the home, mobile phones belong to one person and are not shared. Also, the cell phone is the one item that we carry with us all the time. As a result, an effective mobile marketing strategy is a great way to let your target customers learn about your new app and where they can purchase it.

DIRECT RESPONSE

Smartphones give us access to text-based communication on the go. This provides companies a new way

Several major airlines are testing Wi-Fi in-flight connectivity, so you may soon be able to reach customers as they travel by air. Some systems allow for laptop and mobile phone connections to the Internet.

to directly market to customers without interrupting the recipient's day. Mobile advertising gives the customer the ability to directly respond to a message sent by an advertiser. Unlike TV and radio commercials, sending a mobile marketing message by text, e-mail, or using a social networking site allows the receiver to directly and immediately access the information about a product or promotion. Successful mobile marketing campaigns ask the consumer to respond

LOCATION-BASED SEARCH

Location-based search (LBS) is when mobile search engines are used to specify your location using GPS technology. It allows the mobile search to be targeted to your exact position. Yelp is a search engine that is using this technology to create a personalized list of businesses that are located where you are at any time. They include reviews of restaurants, shopping, events, and local services, to name a few categories. You can look at the locations of these businesses on a map, check out reviews, and link to the businesses' Web sites for coupons. There is no need to carry around guidebooks when you are in a new city: just use your cell phone to connect you to your new geographic location and provide you with current information.

to the marketing message by signing up for text alerts or going to the advertiser's Web site for more information.

For a small business, mobile marketing can create interest in a new product. For example, if you are an app developer attending a conference in Atlanta, Georgia, you can send an e-mail and text message to your client base living in the Atlanta area to inform them of the event. You can provide potential customers with the date and time you will be demonstrating your new app and announce that discounts will be available for those who attend the conference and visit your booth.

Mobile marketing allows a business to reach its customers and potential customers via mobile devices, and the recipients consume the marketing message when it is convenient for them. The technology that runs smartphones and computer tablets is constantly changing and becoming more efficient. This will enhance the quality and speed of the voice, data, and multimedia functions on these devices in the years to come.

CHAPTER 5

CREATIVE THINKING

Thinking of something new is what creates innovation and change. When you are looking for ways to promote your product, you need to experiment with different ways of attracting customers and finding people eager to suggest your product to others. Being open-minded and engaging will create new opportunities for you and your business.

Seek new people and new experiences when attending conferences, traveling, or in informal social settings. Networking with people outside your field is just as important as connecting with people in your field. A creative idea or concept can arise when you step outside the box.

Instead of using the same methods over and over to market your products, break your routine. You may think that the gaming app you created will appeal only to males between the ages of sixteen and twenty-four, but you may find that young women are potential customers, too. Why not demonstrate your app at a shopping mall where women shop? You may be surprised at the response you get from a new audience. It is important to focus on your target customer base, but it is also critical

Most consumers are willing to try something new if it is for free. Offering a free version of your mobile app will create interest in your product.

to expand your customer profile by reaching out to new markets.

KNOW YOUR CUSTOMERS

Another way to be creative is to watch the behavior of potential customers. Carmine Gallo, author of *The Innovation Secrets of Steve Jobs*, says that innovators watch people carefully and discover breakthroughs while observing others. Especially when thinking of the next successful iPad or iPhone app, you need to watch and listen to find out what people want or what they are trying to accomplish, and provide them with an easy and efficient way to do it. Simply watching your classmates use their computers or work on a project may trigger a new idea for a product or app. Look at your product through the consumers' eyes, and design your marketing to show how they can use the item you are selling.

Large companies use advertising agencies and marketing firms to conduct market research. They use focus groups to analyze what customers are looking for in products and what makes them pick the products they choose. You don't need to spend the money on these services if you are constantly observing and reaching out to your customers. If you are involved with your potential customers online through social media and blogs, and in person at conventions and meetings, then you already know a great deal about what your customers want.

Follow us on twitter

www.twitter.com/gamescomcologne

When scanned with a smartphone camera, a QR (quick response) code automatically connects to online text, photos, music, and URLs. Small businesses can generate their own QR codes and use them in their marketing.

CREATE YOUR OWN QR CODE

Quick response codes (QR codes) are small, square dot-matrix bar codes that are popping up everywhere these days. These codes are captured by a cell phone camera and decoded by software installed on the phone. A QR code may open a Web site, send a text message, or download a coupon. These codes were originally created in 1994 by a subsidiary of Toyota, Denso Wave, to track vehicles during the manufacturing process. Now, they are found in magazines, on product packaging, and on signs everywhere. They are used to redirect a consumer to information about a product or service. Many smartphones are entering the market with the software to read QR codes preinstalled.

You may need to get out of your regular surroundings to make effective observations about what your customers want. Head to the school library, neighborhood coffee house with Wi-Fi, or shopping mall to connect with consumers and watch their habits. Remember that imagination and creativity are the keys to success. Be confident enough to think differently. Try new things, both in inventing new products and in discovering ways to market them to your customers.

WORKING HARD PAYS OFF

If you want to be a successful entrepreneur, you need to provide a quality product and keep your standards high in everything you do. If you try to rush the release of a new app that is not ready for market, you will damage your reputation as a developer. A commitment to excellence is what made Steve Jobs, Apple cofounder and CEO, a successful leader and innovator. The commitment to excellence extends past the product into every aspect of your business.

Your Web site, sales efforts, and customer service all need to be the best they can be. Marketing your product is just as important as creating the product. There may be hundreds of game apps available, but you need to explain to consumers why your app is the one to buy. In a crowded field, like game apps, your goal is to set your product apart from the others in its category. This requires that you articulate what makes your app unique and tailor that message to your target audience.

FOLLOW YOUR DREAMS

Many successful entrepreneurs had an "aha" moment of discovery and innovation when they thought about how they could change something that already existed. In his book, Gallo focuses on three success stories: Apple, Starbucks, and Cranium, Inc., the company that created the board game Cranium. Gallo points out that the individual innovators in these companies did not discuss their business successes in terms of the products they sold. They each found success in the void they filled for the consumer. Howard Schultz, CEO and chairman of Starbucks, talks about Starbucks as a destination between home and work that happens to sell coffee. Cranium became one of the fastest-selling board games in history because it allows everyone to have a chance to shine. In Gallo's words: "Apple is not in the computer business; it is in the business of unleashing your personal creativity."

Starbucks did not invent the coffee shop, and Apple did not invent the computer. These companies took these products to a new level by focusing on the customer experience, not the product. If you have a passion for a new idea, you can turn it into a profitable product by following your dreams and caring about your potential customers. Put yourself in the position of the customer who is going to buy your product, and make your decisions about design, functionality, and marketing based on the user's perspective.

KEEP IT SIMPLE

Have you heard the expression "Don't bite off more than you can chew"? Obviously, this means don't fill your mouth with too much food, but it can pertain to your business as well. You can set yourself up for failure if you take on too much, too soon. Don't expand your business before you have mastered what you already have on your plate. Ask yourself the following questions:

1. Can you manage your current product line, including updates?

2. Are you able to answer all customer concerns in a timely manner?

3. Do you update your Web site, Twitter feed, and Facebook page on a regular basis?

If you answered yes to all of these questions, then you can entertain the idea of expanding your product line. If you answered no to any of the questions above, you should stick to what you are already producing. Stay focused on creating one product with a satisfied customer base.

Only diversify your product line if you have something new and noteworthy to add. Many businesses make the mistake of doing too many things but not doing any of them well. Remember that quality is more important than quantity. Your reputation as an entrepreneur depends on your ability to keep your products up-to-date and operating the way consumers expect them to.

Discipline is the key to becoming an efficient businessperson. Focus on creating a Web site that is easy to navigate, and link your Web site to your social networking pages. Most people don't like to read long descriptions or instructions on how to use a new product. Keep your communications simple and easy to understand. Consumers looking for new apps have short attention spans. Reach out to them by telling them what makes your app useful and helpful.

Focus your marketing plan on the likely users of your product. Identify where and how they make their purchases. A successful entrepreneur is always looking for needs and

When Apple introduced the iPad, it was the only featured product on Apple's home page. Learn from Apple and focus on your latest product. Make it easy to download or order your product on your Web site. A simple process and easy customer experience should be your goal.

DO WHAT YOU LOVE

Entrepreneurs who have achieved success will consistently tell you that they are doing what they love. Passion for your work and work product is what keeps you going when things don't go your way. You will face rejection, exhaustion, and frustration at times when you are trying to achieve your goals, but passion for what you are doing will help you persist. It will take an enormous amount of time and energy to create a business that you will be proud of, and that means you will need to be realistic about your goals.

Digital entrepreneurs need to learn to navigate a complicated marketing landscape that is changing every day as the technology and tools are constantly evolving. Today, online communication is where we all go to socialize, get information, and market products and services. As a digital entrepreneur, you need to have a marketing plan to reach your target audience online. To increase your sales, you need to have a presence on the social media sites that your potential customers use most. Building your online identity for your company and product is critical to a successful digital business.

GLOSSARY

BANNER An advertisement displayed on a Web page or mobile Web page, usually above, below, or to the side of the page's main content.

BLOG A regularly updated Web site with individual posts that are displayed in reverse chronological order.

CPM Cost per mille, or cost per thousand impressions; the amount an advertiser pays for every thousand instances an advertisement is shown online.

GPS Global positioning system; a radio navigation system that determines a user's exact location.

MARKETING The process of promoting, selling, and distributing a product or service, including seeking, reaching, and satisfying the target customer.

MICROBLOGGING A form of blogging that allows users to send and receive short text updates. Twitter is a popular microblogging site.

MOBILE MARKETING A set of practices that allows businesses to communicate with their target audiences, often in an interactive way, through mobile devices and networks.

OPEN SOURCE SOFTWARE Software for which the source code is made publicly available to allow for modification.

PAY-PER-CLICK (PPC) A form of online advertising in which businesses are charged for their advertisement each time someone clicks on it.

QR CODE Quick response code; a bar code that can be read from a mobile device by taking its picture with a digital camera.

SDK Software development kit; a set of development tools used to create an application for a specific operating system.

SEARCH ENGINE MARKETING (SEM) Advertising on a search engine, such as Google or Yahoo!.

TECHNORATI An online blog directory that organizes tagged blog posts by category.

URL Universal resource locator; the address of a World Wide Web page.

VLOG A blog that is made up of video material.

WEB TRAFFIC The amount of visitors and visits a Web site receives.

Advancing Canadian Entrepreneurship (ACE)

266 King Street West, Suite 403
Toronto, ON M5V 1H8
Canada
(800) 766-8169
Web site: http://www.acecanada.ca
ACE is a campus-based youth entrepreneurship organization dedicated to teaching and inspiring young Canadians to create brighter futures for themselves and their communities.

CTIA – The Wireless Association

1400 16th Street NW, Suite 600
Washington, DC 20036
(202) 736-3200
Web site: http://www.ctia.org
This international nonprofit membership organization represents the wireless communication industry. Members include wireless carriers and their suppliers, as well as providers and manufacturers of wireless data services and products. CTIA organizes trade shows and provides certification programs.

Entrepreneurs' Organization (EO)

500 Montgomery Street, Suite 700
Alexandria, VA 22314
(703) 519-6700
Web site: http://www.eonetwork.org
This global network of business owners enables entrepreneurs to learn and grow from each other, leading to greater business success and an enriched personal life.

International Game Developers Association (IGDA)
19 Mantua Road
Mount Royal, NJ 08061
(856) 423-2990
Web site: http://www.igda.org
IGDA is a nonprofit membership organization that serves individuals who create video games. They bring together developers at conferences, in local chapters, and in special interest groups to improve their lives and craft.

Mobile Marketing Association (MMA)
P.O. Box 3963
Bellevue, WA 98009-3963
(646) 257-4515
Web site: http://www.mmaglobal.com
The Mobile Marketing Association (MMA) is a nonprofit trade association that works to promote, educate, measure, guide, and protect the mobile marketing industry worldwide. The organization publishes the *International Journal of Mobile Marketing*.

WEB SITES

Due to the changing nature of Internet links, Rosen Publishing has developed an online list of Web sites related to the subject of this book. This site is updated regularly. Please use this link to access the list:

http://www.rosenlinks.com/deaa/twee

FOR FURTHER READING

Cohen, David G., and Brad Feld. *Do More Faster: TechStars Lessons to Accelerate Your Startup*. Hoboken, NJ: Wiley, 2011.

Dannen, Chris, and Christopher White. *Beginning iOS Apps with Facebook and Twitter APIs for iPhone, iPad, and iPod Touch*. New York, NY: Apress, 2011.

Evans, Liana. *Social Media Marketing: Strategies for Engaging in Facebook, Twitter, & Other Social Media*. Indianapolis, IN: Que, 2010.

Ford, Jerry Lee. *Scratch Programming for Teens*. Boston, MA: Course Technology, 2009.

Habgood, Jacob, and Mark H. Overmars. *The Game Maker's Apprentice: Game Development for Beginners*. New York, NY: Apress, 2006.

Jackson, Wallace. *Android Apps for Absolute Beginners*. New York, NY: Apress, 2011.

Kerpen, Dave. *Likeable Social Media: How to Delight Your Customers, Create an Irresistible Brand, and Be Generally Amazing on Facebook (& Other Social Networks)*. New York, NY: McGraw-Hill, 2011.

Lewis, Rory. *iPhone and iPad Apps for Absolute Beginners*. New York, NY: Apress, 2010.

Martin, Chuck. *The Third Screen: Marketing to Your Customers in a World Gone Mobile*. Boston, MA: Nicholas Brealey Publishing, 2011.

McWade, John. *Before & After: How to Design Cool Stuff*. Berkeley, CA: Peachpit, 2010.

Pipes, Alan. *How to Design Websites*. London, England: Laurence King, 2011.

Ramsey, Dave. *EntreLeadership: 20 Years of Practical Business Wisdom from the Trenches*. New York, NY: Howard Books, 2011.

Salt, Simon. *Social Location Marketing: Outshining Your Competitors on Foursquare, Gowalla, Yelp, and Other Location Sharing Sites*. Indianapolis, IN: Que, 2011.

Sethi, Maneesh. *Web Design for Teens*. Boston, MA: Course PTR, 2004.

Sethi, Maneesh, and Eric Grebler. *3D Game Programming for Teens*. 2nd ed. Boston, MA: Course Technology/ Cengage Learning, 2009.

Sobhany, Rana June. *Mobilize: Strategies for Success from the Frontlines of the App Revolution*. Philadelphia, PA: Vanguard Press, 2011.

Tyler, Jason. *Google App Inventor for Android: Build Your Own Apps—No Experience Required!* Hoboken, NJ: John Wiley, 2011.

Yarmosh, Ken. *App Savvy: Turning Ideas into iPad and iPhone Apps Customers Really Want*. Sebastopol, CA: O'Reilly, 2011.

Zechner, Mario. *Beginning Android Games*. New York, NY: Apress, 2011.

BIBLIOGRAPHY

Becker, Michael, and John Arnold. *Mobile Marketing for Dummies*. Hoboken, NJ: Wiley, 2010.

Chen, Brian X. "iPhone Developers Go from Rags to Riches." Wired.com, September 19, 2008. Retrieved October 5, 2011 (http://www.wired.com/gadgetlab/2008/09/indie-developer).

Dunay, Paul, and Richard Krueger. *Facebook Marketing for Dummies*. Hoboken, NJ: Wiley, 2010.

Gallo, Carmine. *The Innovation Secrets of Steve Jobs: Insanely Different Principles for Breakthrough Success*. New York, NY: McGraw-Hill, 2011.

Gwozdz, Dave. "Don't Cut Corners When Creating for Mobile, It's a Different Medium." AdAge.com, November 29, 2011. Retrieved December 3, 2011 (http://adage.com/article/digitalnext/cut-corners-ads-mobile-a-unique-medium/231214/).

Hughes, Jeffrey F. *iPhone & iPad Apps Marketing: Secrets to Selling Your iPhone and iPad Apps*. Indianapolis, IN: Que Publishing, 2010.

Krum, Cindy. *Mobile Marketing: Finding Your Customers No Matter Where They Are*. Indianapolis, IN: Que, 2010.

Mathieson, Rick. *The On-Demand Brand: 10 Rules for Digital Marketing Success in an Anytime, Everywhere World*. New York, NY: AMACOM, 2010.

Prince, Dennis L. *Get Rich with Twitter: Harness the Power of the Twitterverse and Reach More Customers Than Ever Before*. New York, NY: McGraw-Hill, 2010.

Rich, Jason, and J. S. McDougall. *Start Your Own Blogging Business: Generate Income from Advertisers, Subscribers, Merchandising, and More*. 2nd ed. Irvine, CA: J. L. Calmes, 2010.

Rogers, David L. *The Network Is Your Customer: Five Strategies to Thrive in a Digital Age*. New Haven, CT: Yale University Press, 2010.

Stelzner, Michael. "2011 Social Media Marketing Industry Report." *Social Media Examiner*, April 2011. Retrieved October 5, 2011 (http://www.socialmediaexaminer.com/social-media-marketing-industry-report-2011/).

Treadaway, Chris, and Mari Smith. *Facebook Marketing: An Hour a Day*. Indianapolis, IN: Wiley Publishing, 2010.

INDEX

ABOUT THE AUTHOR

Suzanne Weinick earned a bachelor of arts degree from the University at Albany, State University of New York, with a major in political science and a minor in communications. Weinick went on to Hofstra University School of Law and practiced corporate law full-time until she became a mom. She now enjoys writing books for tweens and teens. She has a computer geek husband who has taught her how to use the Internet and social networking sites. She also has a seventeen-year-old daughter and fourteen-year-old son who help her hone her computer skills.

PHOTO CREDITS

Cover, p. 1 (globe) © iStockphoto.com/pixitive; cover, p. 1 (apps) © iStockphoto.com/Merve Karahan; pp. 3, 4–5 (numbers, laptops) © iStockphoto.com/loops7; pp. 4–5 (inset image) Jupiterimages/Photos.com/Thinkstock; pp. 5 (bottom), 8, 19, 28, 39, 46 © iStockphoto.com/Dennis Glorie; p. 6 LWA/Riser/Getty Images; pp. 9, 13, 21 Bloomberg/Getty Images; p. 11 AFP/Newscom; p. 24 © David J. Green-lifestyle themes/Alamy; p. 27 © NetPhotos/Alamy; pp. 29, 37, 40 © AP Images; p. 30 © incamerastock/Alamy; p. 32 Brendan O'Sullivan/Photolibrary; p. 43 EyesWideOpen/Getty Images; p. 47 © Joyce Marshall/Fort Worth Star-Telegram/MCT/ZUMA Press; p. 48 © Jochen Tack/Alamy; p. 53 Robert Nickelsberg/Getty Images; interior background image (glitter) © iStockphoto.com/Tobias Helbig; remaining interior background image © iStockphoto.com/Alexander Putyata.

Designer: Brian Garvey; Editor: Andrea Sclarow Paskoff; Photo Researcher: Amy Feinberg